THE MYSTERY OF ROBERT EMMET'S GRAVE

ROBERT EMMET from an engraving by H. Brocas.
Photograph by permission of Director of National Library of Ireland.

THE Mystery OF ROBERT EMMET'S Grave

A Fascinating Story of Deception, Intrigue and Misunderstanding

by

MICHAEL BARRY

Saturn Books, Fermoy, Co. Cork.

By the same author:

No Flowers By Request & Other Stories
Poems For your Pleasure
The Romance of Sarah Curran
An Affair of Honour (Irish Duels & Duelists)
The Story of Cork Airport.
The International Aviation Quiz Book. Vol. 1
By Pen and Pulpit. (Life & Times of the Author Canon Sheehan).

ISBN 0 9515387 2 1

Cover – Engraving of Robert Emmet by Brocas (Courtesy Nat. Library)

Printed by Litho Press Co., Midleton, Co. Cork.

CONTENTS

Illustrations

Acknowledgements

Sincere thanks to the Staffs of the National Library, Dublin; The Cork Co. Library (Reference Section) and The Representative Church Body Library, Dublin for their assistance and also to Lieut. Cdr. Niall Brunicardi for his advice and help with the proofs.

The illustrations used in this book were from the following sources:

Robert Emmet – Courtesy National Library of Ireland; **Dr. Robert Emmet** (Father of Robert), **Casino** (The Emmet Country Home), **Thomas Addis Emmet, Anne Devlin, House in which Robert Emmet was arrested, Uninscribed Tombstone** (St. Michan's Churchyard), **Supposed Emmet Grave** (Old Glasnevin Churchyard), **Site of Emmet Family Vault** (St. Peter's Churchyard), – *Donahoes Magazine*; **Death Mask of Robert Emmet, Dr. Thomas Addis Emmet** – *Incidents From My Life* by Dr. T.A. Emmet; **Robert Holmes** – *Robert Emmet, his Birth Place and Burial* by D.A. Quaid; **Sketch of entrance to Trevor Vault** – (St. Paul's Churchyard) from *Evening Telegraph* Jan. 3rd 1906. **Kilmainham Gaol** – *The Dublin Penny Journal.*

INTRODUCTION

When Robert Emmet, following his abortive rebellion, was tried, found guilty and sentenced to death at Greenstreet Courthouse in Dublin on Monday 19th September 1803, he delivered an impassioned speech from the dock which ranked as one of the greatest ever made under such circumstances. It was a speech that stirred the hearts of countless generations of Irish people. His closing words were as follows:

> "Let my memory be left in oblivion and my tomb remain uninscribed until other times and other men can do justice to my character. When my country takes her place among the nations of the earth, then and not 'til then let my epitaph be written. I have done."

It is close on 190 years since those words were uttered and we ask ourselves what are their relevance in the Ireland of today? We find the answer in the fact that Ireland has certainly taken her place among the nations of the earth; that she is very much part of the international scene both commercially and politically and is both a member of the United Nations and of the European Community. Is it not time therefore to fulfil Robert Emmet's request made in the closing lines of his speech and write his epitaph? There is a snag of course. Where is his uninscribed tomb?

Robert Emmet is the only leader of the United Irishmen period whose final resting place remains a mystery. A number of churchyards laid claim to holding his remains. The Emmet family descendants have had handed down to them the story that the remains lie in the family vault in St. Peter's Churchyard in Aungier Street, Dublin although there is very little proof to substantiate it.

This book examines in great detail the searches that were undertaken down through the years to try and locate Emmet's remains in those churchyards. They were carried out in the mid 1830s, in 1880 and in 1903, the centenary year of Emmet's execution. The results finally discounted the claims of the locations put forward and also failed to establish in any way that

Robert Emmet's remains lay in the family vault in St. Peter's Churchyard.

Because of this, I have now set out to show that the Emmet family never really knew, following the execution, where Robert Emmet's final resting place was but accepted and handed on the plausible story that his remains were finally laid in the family vault.

There was something very sinister regarding the disappearance of Emmet's remains. It is my firm belief that they were never placed in their final resting place by any of this family or friends but that there was a deliberate plot by the Dublin Castle authorities of the day to hide the remains, thus preventing his epitaph from ever being written and his tomb inscribed.

It is my firm belief too that the Irish patriot's headless remains were removed at the dead of night from the pauper's grave in Kilmainham where they had been placed for a brief period and then secretly transported to a location where it was felt they would never be found.

How wrong they were. This book tells of the million to one chance over eighty years later which resulted in the discovery of a headless body in the private vault of the notorious Dr. Edward Trevor who had been Medical Superintendent of Kilmainham at the time of Emmet's incarceration there and who was also a spy for the Castle. The remains on examination matched those of Robert Emmet in size and in age etc. As will be seen no one was better placed to perpetrate this outrage.

It is a story of deception and intrigue that makes fascinating reading, leading one to the firm conclusion that the headless remains are those of the Irish patriot, and as his grand-nephew Dr. T.A. Emmet of New York wrote in 1915,

> It would require but a trifling corroboration from some other source to establish a complete chain of circumstantial evidence to prove that at last the remains of Robert Emmet have been located.

Somewhere among the historical papers of that period the final piece of evidence may exist that would prove conclusively that the remains in the Trevor vault are those of Emmet.

The purpose of my book therefore is that, having related this fascinating story, it will highlight both the importance and urgency of carrying out extensive research to find the missing jig-saw part so that at last Robert Emmet's epitaph can be written and his tomb inscribed. Such tribute is long overdue.

Michael Barry.

Chapter 1

EMMET'S BACKGROUND AND THE ABORTIVE REBELLION

To understand the mystery surrounding the whereabouts of Robert Emmet's grave and the many aspects of that troubled period of Irish history it is necessary first of all to look at his family and at the tragic events which led to his execution on Tuesday 20th September 1803.

Robert Emmet was born in Dublin in 1778, the youngest son of Dr. Robert Emmet who, as a medical man had worked in Cork's North Infirmary for some years and devoted a great part of his time to the poor of the city. The Emmet family lived at Dunscombe's Marsh. Mrs. Elizabeth Emmet was formerly Elizabeth Mason whose family lived in the Ballydowney area near Killarney. The Emmet family moved to Dublin in 1770 when Dr. Emmet took up the post of State Physician there. They were comfortably off and while in Cork held a long lease on a farm some four miles outside of Inchigela. In order to take up the Dublin appointment Dr. Emmet had to pay one thousand pounds, a very considerable sum in those days. He therefore put his house and farm on the market to raise the cash. From accounts of that time it would appear that he had difficulty in the quick disposal of the properties.

However, Dr. Emmet took up the position of State Physician on the 6th March 1770 and the family moved to Dublin. Referring to his departure from Cork, the Board of the North Infirmary thanked him "for the great care that he had taken of the patients" during his time at the Infirmary.

There were seventeen children in the Emmet family and all

DR. ROBERT EMMET – father of Robert Emmet.

except four, three boys and a girl died either at birth or shortly afterwards. In fact Robert was the fifth born in the family to bear his father's name, the latter being extremely keen to have the name perpetuated. The other members of the family who survived into manhood were Christopher Temple, Thomas Addis and Mary Anne.

When the family first moved to Dublin their home was in Molesworth Street. After some time they moved to the West side of St. Stephen's Green, a large imposing building which was beautifully furnished. After a few years they again moved, this time to a large house called "Casino" on about thirteen acres of land located at Milltown, some six miles south of the city. It was there that Robert Emmet was born. The family were society people and although of the Protestant faith, Dr. Emmet was very supportive of things Irish and of Catholic Emancipation. His views rubbed off on two of his sons Robert and Thomas Addis, the latter being a member of the United Irishmen.

Robert Emmet entered Trinity College, Dublin on the 7th October 1793. He was then only fifteen years of age. He was of a shy disposition and did not distinguish himself as a student. Where languages and science were concerned he was reasonably competent. While in College he became a close friend of Thomas Moore the poet and with Richard Curran who was then studying law there and with whose sister Sarah, Robert had a romantic attachment some years later.

He never participated greatly in any historical debate while at Trinity except when the name of Ireland came up. Then he would make a very generous contribution. Debates on the political situation in Ireland at that time were prohibited in the College. While there he secretly enrolled in a branch of the Society of United Irishmen which had been reconstituted. Trinity was strongly opposed to this type of activity and moves were made to expel the students who joined. Rather than be expelled, he left Trinity "taking his name off the books."

Robert Emmet was too young to have had any involvement in the 1798 rebellion. His brother Thomas Addis Emmet had joined the United Irishmen in 1792 and because of his involvement with

Casino, The Country Place of Dr. Robert Emmet

them was imprisoned at Fort George in Scotland. Robert was full of admiration for the United Irishmen and visited his brother while there in 1800. A surviving description of Robert Emmet from that time was of "a small wiry young man about five and a half feet high with a sallow slightly pockmarked face, grey heavy lidded eyes, small and searching with a prominent straight thin nose."

The animosity displayed towards many United Irishmen in prison in Ireland following the failure of the 1798 rebellion was very great and Kilmainham was the scene for much of this. It is important to bear this in mind in the context of the story as it unfolds, and with regard to the ferocity with which punishment was often meted out to many prisoners.

It will be seen later that the abortive rebellion was to catch the imagination of the Irish people more than anything that had gone before it, its leader writing himself into the pages of Irish history. Because of this the location of his remains would be a secret well worth keeping by the authorities and the events leading up to his execution paved the way for this extraordinary occurrence. Were it not for the disappearance of Emmet's body, there is no doubt that his grave would have become the most hallowed in the country.

Following the defeat of the United Irishmen in 1798 a new movement was spearheaded to take its place. Robert Emmet was not as he himself was to say later "the head and life's blood of this rebellion" but he was certainly the front man. He went to the Continent in 1801 to study revolution having been sent there on the instructions of the Executive Directory of the United Irishmen. There he met many great men of the period such as Tallyrand and Napoleon. Being a member of Irish Society gave him entree to "the salons of aristocrats and intelligentsia."

Towards the end of July 1802 his brother Thomas Addis Emmet was released from Fort George prison in Scotland and sent to the Continent where his wife Jane joined him. Robert was about to return home from there around that time and he met them both in Brussels. He was returning to Ireland rather urgently. Some say he had received a false message suggesting that he come back as soon as possible to lay the foundations for a new rebellion. He discussed his plans and the political situation in Ireland with his brother and it is understood that both Thomas Addis and his wife pleaded earnestly with him to desist from the path he was proposing to take. Their pleas were in vain and Robert Emmet was back again in Dublin in October 1802. It was thought that even then the Castle authorities knew what he was planning and had him under observation.

In December of that year 1802 his father died leaving him a legacy of between two and three thousand pounds, money he would later use to help his planned rebellion. His family left their Milltown home in March 1803 and moved nearer town to Donnybrook. By now he was deeply involved in plans for an uprising and he did not move with them. Instead he took lodgings with a family called Palmer at Harolds Cross staying there under the name of Hewit. He later moved from there and rented a house at Butterfield Lane in the same area under the name of Ellis. There Anne Devlin became his housekeeper.

Robert Emmet's plans were hampered from the outset by varying circumstances, many of them outside his control. The British authorities were adamant that there would be no repeat of the 1798 rebellion and were consequently infiltrating those involved in the planning of an insurrection, thus gathering as much information as possible. Emmet himself was a young man of very high principles but this however didn't count with many of his so-called supporters, some of whom were in reality spies. The support that he had hoped to get from about five thousand was gradually being eroded through the spy network of the Castle authorities. Many of those actively plotting against his endeavours to stage a rebellion had at one time been United Irishmen themselves and had now turned informers. As a result of all this the authorities were well briefed as to what was going on.

Emmet's plan was to attack and take Dublin Castle. If that was successful then he hoped that the rebellion would spread out from the city and attract support from the neighbouring counties such as Wicklow. His preparations were not without incident. He

THOMAS ADDIS EMMET – brother of Robert Emmet.

had arms depots scattered about the city in properties he had rented and in one of them an explosion took place on the 16th July wrecking the depot and killing one man. Under normal circumstances the authorities would have been on the scene immediately but decided to take no action whatever, pretending to ignore the incident, not wanting to scare Emmet and his men but hoping that they would eventually be trapped.

By now Robert Emmet was very nervous at the turn of events. Things were not going according to plan for him. He therefore decided to move as quickly as possible in getting the rebellion under way. Saturday evening of the 23rd July 1803 was chosen. It was market day in Dublin and it was felt that as the streets would be thronged with tradesmen and labourers, the assembly of rebels at various points wouldn't be noticed. The authorities themselves were by this time beginning to get anxious at the news being fed to them through their network of spies and informers.

At 9p.m. on the evening of 23rd July Emmet decided to make his move. He was totally frustrated and his dream of being at the head of thousands of Irishmen was shattered. It was in fact a nightmare as he had less than one hundred trusted men to do battle by his side. Most of the Dublin men had refused to rise with him when the time came and those from Kildare had gone home. To give the lead to those who would follow him he put on white pantaloons and a white waistcoat over which he wore a green coat with golden epaulettes. Around his waist was a crimson sash from which hung a brace of pistols and at his side was a sword. To complete his dress he wore a beaver cocked hat with white feathers and on his feet were hessian boots.

That was the appearance of Robert Emmet when he came out on to Thomas Street from Marshalsea Lane. Some of those with him had firearms while other had pikes. They looked a motley crew and the addition to their ranks of some drunkards and ruffians who poured out of the taverns just to rob and plunder was the last thing that Emmet wanted. Their behaviour later in the evening really increased the gravity of the offense of insurrection.

There had been a complete mix up of the planned time of the

rebellion. On that fateful evening there was a lot of activity in the Marshalsea Lane area as many of the carters had an inkling of what was afoot and thus were anxious to get away with their loads as soon as possible. All this activity was mistaken by the lookout man for the approach of the army and he immediately raised the alarm. It was a fatal mistake that triggered off the insurrection before the actual time intended. Emmet now seeing that all was lost and the situation hopeless addressed those who followed him in to Francis Street. There were many he knew who couldn't be relied upon and realising this he told them that any attempt to capture the Castle under the present circumstances was bound to fail and that it was better they moved out to the Wicklow hills until a more favourable situation developed. This was not what many of them wanted and so they took off, grouping into armed gangs much to Emmet's disgust. Many were killed as they took on soldiers here and there in the city and some behaved in a rather savage way.

Emmet's glorious rebellion had by now become just an excuse for violence and death and he was powerless to stop it. One of the worst escapades of the armed gangs was the brutal murder of the Lord Chief Justice, Lord Kilwarden. He was travelling in to the city from his home in Lyons, Co. Kildare accompanied by his daughter and nephew when their carriage was attacked and both men were piked to death. The authorities were now given good reason to hunt down not alone those who perpetrated the murders but also Emmet who instigated the rebellion. He was a wanted man with a price on his head. In all of the skirmishes, over thirty of the rebels were killed and many soldiers also lost their lives. The entire outbreak lasted only about three hours and was a total disaster.

Emmet and some of his trusted men had fled the scene and hid that first night at his house at Butterfield Lane. His housekeeper Anne Devlin was there and on the following morning they slipped out and went to her father's house where they were fed and given beds for the night. On Sunday afternoon they moved again and stayed at different locations for a few days. Eventually Emmet and his men agreed that their best course of

The house in which Robert Emmet was arrested.

action would be for each man to look out for his own safety and take whatever evasive action he felt necessary. Robert Emmet slipped back to Rathfarnham to be near his girl friend Sarah Curran and stayed in lodgings at the home of Mrs. Palmer at Harold's Cross. It will be recalled that he had stayed there previously before he got his own place and again as on the previous occasion he gave his name as Hewit.

One of those who suffered most where Emmet's abortive rising was concerned was Anne Devlin. She had been picked up a few days after the rebellion and closely questioned as to the whereabouts of the rebels. She firmly resisted this pressure and was therefore tortured and half hanged from the shafts of a horse cart. Yet she never yielded any information on Emmet's whereabouts. She was then taken to the Coombe guardhouse where she was kept for a few days before being released.

As Emmet couldn't be traced she was arrested again and brought to Dublin Castle where she was offered all kinds of bribes including five hundred pounds if she revealed the whereabouts of Emmet and his men. She steadfastly refused this large sum and consequently was lodged with all her family in Kilmainham with the exception of a boy and a little girl. The Medical Superintendent of Kilmainham then was the ill-famed Dr. Trevor whose name will play a large part in this story in a later chapter of this book. Anne Devlin was kept in very harsh conditions in that gaol until she was released on 8th March 1806.

Hundreds of men had been arrested following Emmet's rebellion, some on only very slight suspicion and thrown into prison. Many to save their own necks turned informer and gave information which led to the arrest of others. Some chose to fight their arrest and engaged barristers. One of those engaged was Leonard McNally. Sadly they didn't know he was a spy who passed all the information given him in confidence to Dublin Castle authorities. McNally was one of the most trusted men in the United Irishmen movement yet he was probably one of the most notorious spies in that period of Irish history, responsible for the arrests and subsequent deaths of many of his fellow Irishmen. He was known as "McNally the Incorruptible" during the United

ANNE DEVLIN

Irishmen period and being a member of that body, he entertained many of the rebel leaders and then passed everything he had learned to the Castle.

Robert Emmet was the big fish the authorities wanted in their net and around the middle of August there was a reward of three hundred pounds for his arrest. He had been staying in the Palmer household until the 25th August when he was discovered. Someone definitely had betrayed him and it wasn't Mrs. Palmer. The betrayer had been reputed to have received one thousand pounds for his work and the man who arrested him got three hundred. There are no definite facts as to who was responsible but in an account book of the Secret Service covering that period and under the date 4th November 1803 there is an entry which reads:

Finlay and Co. Acc. of Richard Jones (to be replaced to the account hereafter) £1000."

Finaly and Co. were bankers.

In Anne Devlin's *Life* by Luke Cullen there are interesting facts that throw some light on this matter. Anne Devlin related that

> "old Doyle of Ballinameece and an idiot son of his were in Kilmainham at this time. It has been observed that it was at this man's house Mr. Emmet and his staff stopped the night they left my father's. At this time, there was a warrant issued for the apprehension of another son of Doyle's who was accused of robbing a Mr. Ormsby near Tallaght. A Mr. Jones from the quarter used to visit Doyle in prison and I was informed by Wm. Kearney's wife that it was through Jones's influence that Doyle was not proceeded against. But Doyle had another son Simon who kept a public house at Harold's Cross and used to go messages and supplied Mr. Emmet with butter and eggs while he was at Mrs. Palmer's."

In her book *The Pursuit of Robert Emmet* Helen Landreth says that probably Anne Devlin meant that Simon Doyle went on messages during Emmet's first stay at the Palmers' and that he would have known Emmet from those transactions. Also she states that there was a local tradition that Simon Doyle was delivering some supplies at the Palmers' door on the day of Emmet's capture and caught sight of him inside.

Anne Devlin further related in her account that

"On the day previous to the arrest of Mr. Emmet this Simon Doyle rode to his father's at a very unusual and rapid rate. He was very much noticed by his old neighbours who justly held him in very low estimation. . . . He rode back at the same rate and his old neighbours did not hesitate to say there was something in the wind. Rich'd Jones, who used to visit Doyle in prison was a tenant to Mr. Finlay the banker. He was in a very respectable station in life (a gentleman farmer) and as silky a fellow as old Doyle, who was called Silky Jock for his insinuating disposition. But if Simon Doyle or his father were the persons by whom Mr. Emmet was betrayed, it is certain that they never received the £1000. Jones went to reside in the County Kildare soon after.

Whether one of the Doyles or Richard Jones himself had a connection with Emmet's betrayal is open to conjecture but whoever was responsible gave the police just the break they needed.

Acting on a tip-off, the chief of Secret Police, Major Sirr and one soldier rode out to the Palmers' residence between six and seven on the evening of the 25th August and eventually apprehended Robert Emmet.

An interesting factor in relation to the many informers on the pay roll of the British authorities was the importance they placed on these people. This came to the forefront very shortly after Emmet had been arrested. It was in a letter that Wickham, the Chief Secretary for Ireland wrote to the British Government. Referring to the prospect of bringing Robert Emmet to trial, he said:

> The question of bringing forward secret information has been well confirmed and discussed and there is but one opinion on the subject – viz., that it were a thousand times better that Emmet should escape than that we should close for ever a most accurate source of information.

Robert Emmet was held at Kilmainham and was put under great

pressure at secret examinations regarding the abortive rebellion. His examiners set out to try and destroy his character and his reputation by trying to get him to inform on his colleagues and so brand him as an opportunist and betrayer. In this the authorities failed miserably. Later Emmet wrote to the Chief Secretary offering to discuss his rebellion in a similar way some United Irishmen leaders did in 1798 including his brother Thomas Addis Emmet. This offer was refused. His only hope was to try to escape.

Among the many political prisoners there at that time was his cousin St. John Mason, a barrister. Because of his relationship with Emmet he had been thrown into prison although it was agreed by many connected with the rebellion that Mason hadn't the slightest connection with it and was in fact opposed to it.

The man who was all powerful in Kilmainham at that time was Dr. Trevor and it is of interest to look briefly at this evil man. Although nominally regarded as being the physician in Kilmainham, he also held other positions there. For example he was government overseer or superintendent of the State prisoners. He was a sutler or seller of extra provisions to inmates for a price; he was accountant, magistrate, agent for the distribution of Secret Service money and officer of remuneration for imprisonment etc.

One of his functions in Kilmainham was the examination of prisoners, extracting information from them which he would then pass on to the State prosecutors. These examinations were referred to in the cases of a number of Emmet's associates who had been picked up and later put on trial. Trevor was in fact referred to by one of the witnesses at Emmet's own trial. He was the sole intermediary between Kilmainham gaol and Dublin Castle and an examination of the Secret Service money books shows his name frequently apearing both as principal and as agent and among the "Receipts" for these payments.

In the *Secret Service Money Book* the first entry of his name appears in 1798 where he was described as "Mr. Trevor Royal Infirmary." Trevor's father-in-law also appears in the list under the heading "Mr. Wigelsworth, steward Royal Infirmary."

It was Trevor who interviewed Ann Devlin, housekeeper to

Robert Emmet. Her harsh treatment in Kilmainham is a sad indictment of Trevor's authority there. He was also the prime mover in inveigling Robert Emmet to escape. He had Emmet's letters intercepted and also witheld those which Emmet wrote shortly before his execution and entrusted to him for delivery to his brother Thomas Addis Emmet and to Richard Curran, brother of Sarah. It is a historical fact that Trevor publicly embraced Emmet as the latter was leaving gaol on the way to his execution, having prior to that sold him out to the Castle while he languished in Kilmainham awaiting trial.

Dr. Edward Trevor had been appointed Medical Superintendent of Prisons early in 1797 and was based at Kilmainham. In the years ahead he was to bring about great changes in the prison and become one of the most hated and despised men in the prison service. Within a short time of his appointment he had assumed complete authority, and apart from being a spy himself, he quickly established a network of them within the prison walls. He was feared by staff and inmates and an example of his vile character is worth noting here.

The first gaoler at Kilmainham had been Robert Ware who by all accounts was a kind man. He had been dismissed following the escape of some prisoners and had been replaced by John Richardson who with his wife and three children had an apartment in the prison. In November 1798 he developed a very serious fever and his anxious wife was obliged to call Trevor to the bedside of her extremely ill husband. He refused to come on learning that the gaoler's salary hadn't yet come through and she hadn't the cash available. It was only when the distraught wife offered him a pair of silver mounted pistols in lieu of money that he relented and attended her husband.

Sadly after some days John Richardson died and within hours following his burial Mrs. Richardson came down with the fever and again Dr. Trevor was sent for. His behaviour was precisely the same as on the first occasion. This time she was obliged to give him a horse that belonged to her husband and valued at twenty five pounds, the equivalent of a year's salary for her husband. Mrs. Richardson recovered but Trevor had some unfinished business to undertake. He immediately set out to have her and her children evicted from the gaol. She was obliged to barricade herself and the family in the apartment during Christmas. However, Trevor was eventually successful in obtaining a court order and had them evicted. A measure of the authority he held was shown when he was able to pick his own man as a replacement for John Richardson. The man was George Dunn, already referred to.

Dr. Edward Trevor was a vile man who preyed on public calamity, often remaining in the background while his underlings carried out his evil plans. His activities during the United Irishmen period and that of Robert Emmet have left an indelible mark on the annals of Kilmainham's history. Yet, Trevor was very adept at currying favour where it mattered as for example moving to a fashionable address in Dublin and acting the perfect gentleman. When he died in 1837 he left £36,000, an extremely large sum in those days, a sum which in no way could have been earned from the position he officially held.

Robert Emmet suggested to his cousin St. John Mason that he should offer Dunn a substantial bribe to help him escape. Mason agreed to this and he offered Dunn five hundred pounds to help and should Emmet succeed in escaping another five hundred. Neither Mason or Emmet were aware of the fact that Dunn was passing all the information to Trevor who, as already mentioned, was a spy and therefore relaying it to Dublin Castle.

Dunn and Trevor agreed between themselves to string Mason along for the time being in an effort to get as much information as possible regarding the escape plan. Also, for Dunn to refuse at that stage would mean that he probably would never again gain the confidence of other prisoners and any chance he had of picking up information would dry up.

Dunn went along with the plan for some time and then managed to get himself out of trouble the night the escape was to be attempted. He informed Mason that the plan could fall through if attempted as Trevor whose suspicions were aroused, had removed his quarters to the side of the gaol in which State prisoners were confined. After that the net began to close in further on Robert Emmet and he was arraigned on a charge of high treason on 7th September and his trial was fixed for Monday 19th September at Green Street Courthouse. While awaiting trial his mother died and to add to his misfortune his sister was refused permission to see him.

He engaged the barrister Leonard McNally to defend him not knowing of course that McNally was completely in the payment of the Crown. Emmet also retained another lawyer named Burrows who, as it transpired, was no mean exponent in the passing of information to the Castle. Once they began taking instructions from Emmet for his defence, the confidential information they received was passed on. In the Secret Service records of that period in Ireland it can be seen that McNally got one hundred pounds around the time he agreed to act for Emmet and got a further one hundred pounds two days later.

Robert Emmet's trial at Green Street Courthouse was one of the main talking points in Dublin. The court was presided over by Lord Norbury, the Chief Justice and known as "The Hanging Judge". After the case had been made for and against the plaintiff and the judge had summed up, it was handed over to the jury. Following a brief consultation they brought in a verdict of guilty of treason. When asked by the clerk of the court "What have you therefore now to say, why judgement of death and execution should not be awarded against you according to law," Emmet made a resounding speech, one which to future generations would be known as his 'speech from the dock'. It was something that many generations of Irish people would hear of and read in the years ahead and its closing sentences were:

> "Let my memory be left in oblivion and my tomb remain uninscribed until other times and other men do justice to my character. When my country takes her place among the nations of the earth, then and not 'til then let my epitaph be written.
>
> I have done."

A hushed silence fell on the court as Lord Norbury pronounced sentence on Emmet, death by hanging and then his head to be severed from his body. Following the verdict he was first brought to Newgate prison and given a meal. Shortly after midnight he was returned to Kilmainham, weary and dejected. Later on he was visited by the Rev. Mr. Gamble a clergyman with a view 'to bring his mind to a proper temper and sense of religion.' The clergyman in his report to the authorities said that he had asked Emmet 'how he could reconcile his actions to the Christian principle?' and Emmet had replied that he had expected other resources but found himself entangled with a rabble. Mr. Gamble also gave Holy Communion to the prisoner and joined him in prayer.

To add to the enormous distress that Emmet was under, it was his defence lawyer, McNally the spy, who broke the news to him regarding his mother's recent death. Emmet had asked about her as she had been in very poor health. To his query the traitor pointed his finger upwards and said:

"You will see her this night."

It was the final blow and he then sat down and wrote a farewell letter to his brother Tom and wife Jane and also one to his closest friend Richard Curran, brother of Sarah. Even in those last acts luck was against him. The two letters he had written were never forwarded.

About 1.30p.m. on the 20th September 1803 Robert Emmet was brought from Kilmainham under heavy escort to the place of his execution, a scaffold erected in Thomas Street. There in the presence of a large crowd he was hanged and his head severed from his body. The remains were first brought to Newgate and later that evening to Kilmainham to await the body being claimed. No one claimed it and from there on there was mystery surrounding Robert Emmet's last resting place. It is to this question that the remainder of this book addresses itself.

Chapter Two

THE VANISHED BODY AFTER BURIAL AND THE FIRST SEARCH

In pursuance of official policy Robert Emmet's remains were first brought to Newgate prison and later transferred to Kilmainham. It was customary at that time that the body of an executed person be handed over to relatives if claimed. While the remains of Robert Emmet lay in a thin penal coffin for some hours at Kilmainham, no one claimed them. On the face of things, that may appear to have been an extraordinary situation. Emmet had come from a very well known and highly respected family both socially and politically whose late father had been State Physician.

There were however very good reasons why the body was not claimed. Both of Emmet's parents were by this time deceased and his brother Thomas Addis Emmet was on the Continent. Robert's only sister who was refused permission to see him in prison was in rather poor health and her husband John Patten had been arrested and was in Kilmainham. In fact her brother's tragic death exacerbated her condition to the extent that she died within a year or so. Most other close relatives of Emmet had all been picked up by the authorities following the rebellion and lodged in Kilmainham. With regard to his friends and he had many, not one came forward because by getting involved they would be drawing attention to themselves.

Late in the evening of the 20th September as Robert Emmet's body lay in its thin penal shell at the outer entry of the prison, a very well known Dublin artist named James Petrie called to the gaol seeking permission to make a death mask of Emmet's head. Permission was granted and he took the head away to work in his studio. When he had the task completed he returned with the head to find that by then the coffin with Emmet's body in it was missing.

It was said that Petrie kept the head until a short time before his death when he then gave it to a physician friend of his in Galway. What happened to it from then on is not known. This fact has never been verified. Petrie was a man of very high principles and should he have held on to the head as reported, he most certainly would have made careful provision for its preservation.

In an article on Newgate prison published in a work called *The Picture of Dublin for 1841*, it was stated that some of the keepers had been accused of detaining in their possession the heads and bodies of those executed for high treason to enhance the sums first demanded from their relatives. The article specifically mentions a rumour that Robert Emmet's head was so disposed of. The rumour is also referred to in *Whitelaw's History of Dublin 1818*. The Petrie story however appears to be the one to have been given the greatest credence. It was also stated that the notorious Town Majors, Sirr and Sandys were known to have each been in possession of casts from the Emmet death mask.

Within a short time after his execution, Robert Emmet was immortalised in song and in story, his famous speech from the dock gaining more and more prominence as time passed by. His request that his tomb be left uninscribed until other times etc. prompted the question as where he actually was buried. It became the subject of debate and controversy for many years.

Numerous locations were pointed out as holding Emmet;s remains and it wasn't until 1836 that the first serious search was made to locate the body. This was carried out by Dr. Richard Madden, Fellow of the Royal College of Surgeons, Dublin. The doctor had a very keen interest in that period of Irish history which encompassed the United Irishmen and in fact wrote several volumes on their lives and times. He was also the author of a book *The Memoir of Robert Emmet*. Dr. Madden was a highly respected member of the medical profession in Dublin and set out to make every effort to locate the final resting place of Robert

Death Mask of Robert Emmet

Emmet's remains. He knew very many of his relatives and felt that if any of them had any certain knowledge of where the body of Emmet lay they would have told him and not have allowed him to go on what could be described as a wild good chase.

Early in his searches Dr. Madden made contact with the former gardener to the Emmet family, a man named Leonard. He asked him if he would approach George Dunn whom he knew. The latter had been gaoler of Kilmainham at the time of Emmet's imprisonment there. Madden was anxious to ascertain how the remains of Robert Emmet had been disposed of since no one had claimed them. In due course the information came back from Dunn through Leonard that following execution Emmet's body had eventually been brought to Kilmainham and placed in the outer entry of the prison awaiting someone to claim it. Dunn, he said, had orders that if the body hadn't been claimed within a short time it was to be buried in 'Bully's Acre,' a burial ground at Kilmainham which was also called the 'Hospital Field.' It was there that the remains of executed criminals and paupers were buried.

Dunn had also told Leonard that, not withstanding the order he had received to dispose of the body as quickly as possible, he kept it for several hours expecting that it would be claimed. As already stated it wasn't claimed, which was an indication too of the terror that had been instilled in people at the time of Emmet's abortive rebellion. There was one relative of Emmet's who did escape gaol, a Dr. Powell who was married to a girl named Landon, a cousin of Emmet's. However it was only through remaining in oblivion that he escaped notice and it was therefore inopportune for him to come forward.

As far as Dunn's story was concerned there is little reason to doubt the fact that the burial took place in Bully's Acre. The remains, he related, were buried beside the grave of a man named Felix O'Rourke near the right-hand corner of the burial ground next to the avenue of the Royal Hospital at Kilmainham. Dunn also confirmed what Dr. Madden had already learned namely that someone had called the evening of the execution to make a death mask of Emmet. This man was Petrie.

Uninscribed Tomb – St. Michan's Churchyard

Dr. Madden, in the course of his investigation, was already aware that the remains of Robert Emmet had been removed with great privacy some time after the interment in Bully's Acre and placed elsewhere. This fact was reiterated by Dunn.

It is from this point onwards that all the mystery and controversy arose, several locations laying claim to holding the remains of Emmet. Dr. Madden was unable to elicit from the many contacts he had the whereabouts of the patriot's grave. There appears to have been a conspiracy of silence by the authorities. One prominent theory put forward through the recollections of people around at the time of the execution was that the remains were removed from Bully's Acre and buried in St. Michan's churchyard. This was where the Sheares brothers were buried following their execution. Leonard, the Emmet gardener, was also under that impression. The story was backed up by a man named John Scott. He was a tailor who resided at No. 4 Mitre Alley near Patrick St. It was he in fact who had made Emmet's uniform for the rebellion and uniforms for some of the other leaders. Scott told Leonard that as far as he knew Robert Emmet had been buried in St. Michan's churchyard and that shortly afterwards a very large stone without any inscription on it was laid over the grave.

In contrast to this, it was stated in a small publication *A Memoir of Robert Emmet* by Kinsella that Emmet's remains were brought to St. Anne's churchyard and buried in the grave where his parents had been buried. Robert Emmet's parents had not been buried in St. Annes churchyard. The only member of the family to be buried there was his grandmother, she having died when the family were living in nearby Molesworth Street.

Dr. Madden visited St. Michan's churchyard as a result of Leonard's information and there he saw the stone in question or at least the only stone to match the description given him. It was located about midway on the left hand side of the walk which led from the church to the wall at the extremity of the graveyard. There he found a very large and thick slab lying flat, bearing no inscription, the only uninscribed one in the churchyard. Although he made no effort to have the ground under the slab dug up it would appear from enquiries he made with the church authorities that he was satisfied the remains of Robert Emmet were not there. Confirmation of this will be given later on in the story.

St. Peter's Church in Aungier St. had also been put forward as a possible location for Emmet's remains. This was the burial ground of the Emmet family. Dr. Madden carried out checks there including burial records but also to no avail. All in all, his researches revealed very little and certainly brought him no nearer to finding the final burial place of Robert Emmet. No one of any consequence in that troubled period of Irish history seemed to know and the general consensus among the Emmet dynasty and their relatives was that he was buried in the family vault in St Peter's churchyard.

Robert Emmet's brother Thomas Addis Emmet had by this time been fully settled in America and it was his grandson Dr. Thomas Addis Emmet in later years who was to take the greatest interest in the whereabouts of the patriot's last resting place.

Around 1841 while in New York Dr. Madden visited the Emmet family and gave them as much information as was available to him. As already stated, Madden was the author of the lives of the United Irishmen and apart from being a surgeon he had been appointed by the British authorities as Commissioner and Representative of the negroes in the British West Indies after their emancipation. Dr. Thomas Addis Emmet was then only a boy in New York.

About forty years later in 1880 he however made personal contact with Dr. Madden when he paid a visit to Ireland from New York. Dr. Madden was able to tell him much about the 1798 period of Irish history and also showed him the many places connected with the Emmet family in Dublin. It is of interest to note that from the time Dr. Emmet landed in Cobh until he left Ireland he was under police surveilance. His visit was primarily to investigate the whereabouts if possible of Robert Emmet's last resting place and he later recorded in his autobiography *Incidents of My Life* the investigations he carried out.

There he related also that at the close of the 18th century the Emmets lived on West Stephen's Green and Lamb Lane near the

DR. THOMAS ADDIS EMMET – Grand-Nephew of Robert Emmet

corner of York St. The church of that parish was St. Peter's fronting on Aungier St. The Emmet burial place or family vault had been situated in the churchyard but at the time of Dr. Emmet's visit to Dublin no record or map was available which would define the exact location of the family tomb. Dr. Madden had stated in the second edition of The Lives of the United Irishmen that Robert Emmet's father died at Casino near Milltown in the Autumn of 1802 and that he was buried in the graveyard of St. Peter's Church in Aungier St. on the right hand side of the entrance, "close to the wall on the south side." The tomb or vault had the following inscription:

Here lies the remains of
Robert Emmet, Esq., M.D.,
who died the 9th of December 1802
in the 73rd year of his age.

This of course would certainly place St. Peter's as being a likely place where the remains of Robert Emmet may have been placed should any of his relatives or friends had claimed them in the days or weeks after his initial burial in Bully's Acre. There is however nothing to substantiate that such was the case.

Dr. Thomas Addis Emmet in his 1880 search failed to find either the family tomb or any Emmet grave. He was told by the church authorities that all the tombstones had been removed some years before but were still preserved and that several feet of earth had been spread on the ground's surface to raise it to the level of the street in front. The tombstones, following removal and after the filling in, had been place in piles along the west boundary wall. Dr. Emmet had them carefully examined but none bearing the name of Emmet had been found. As the inscribed stone found by Dr. Madden many years before marking the Emmet vault or tomb was a flat one lying horizontally over the entrance, Dr. Emmet concluded that this had not been removed with the others but was merely covered over when the ground was filled in to the level of Aungier St. and back to White Friar St.

Burial records of the Emmet family in St. Peter's church are as follows: Elizabeth 7th Dec. 1771; Harriet 4th July 1775; Robert 1st May 1786 (this would have been an earlier child than the patriot who had been given the name Robt.); Temple 9th March 1788; Robert 12th December 1802 (the patriot's father); Emilia 11th September 1813.

There are two very important names missing from those Church records. One is Robert Emmet's mother who died shortly before his execution and who was apparently buried with her husband. Robert Emmet's sister (Mrs. Holmes) was also buried in the family vault in St. Peter's churchyard. We shall see further references to these later.

Dr. Thomas Addis Emmet's search in 1880 really gave no clue as to where his grand-uncle's remains had been finally laid.

Chapter 3

THE OBSERVATIONS OF DAVID A. QUAID

In 1902 a Dublin solicitor named David A. Quaid wrote a book called *Robert Emmet – His Birth Place And Burial.* His observations and comments on Emmet's supposed burial place are dealt with here in detail. Many of Mr. Quaid's conclusions were based on speculation and derived from a preconceived idea that Robert Emmet's last resting place was in St. Peter's churchyard in the family vault. However, allowing for that, much of what he wrote was very informative. Mr. Quaid had a detailed knowledge of the Emmet family history, and to get a better picture and understanding of why he as well as the Emmet descendants believed that the family vault in St. Peter's churchyard was the accepted burial place of Robert Emmet's remains, it is worth while to look at what he had to say.

In the main, three churches were in competition as holders of Emmet's remains – St. Peter's Aungier St., St. Michan's Churchyard and Old Glasnevin cemetry. Mr. Quaid set out in a very business-like fashion in his book to come up with a solution and he first looked at who would have been most likely to have had Emmet's remains placed secretly in their last resting place. As mentioned earlier, practically all of Robert Emmet's closest relatives and associates were in prison by the time he had been executed. One of the earliest to be arrested was Robert Holmes, B.L. who was married to Robert Emmet's sister Mary A. Emmet. Holmes had been held in extremely high esteem by Emmet's father. Shortly after Holmes's arrest, St. John Mason, B.L., nephew of Mrs. Emmet and first cousin of Robert was arrested in Nenagh on 9th August 1803 while on circuit there. They were just two of the many relatives or friends picked up and lodged in prison.

Dr. Madden in his writings on the Emmet rebellion mentioned two of Emmet's followers Hope and Dowdall as having escaped to France before his execution. Madden was well informed on these matters and certainly neither of them was State prisoner in 1803. Yet it had been suggested in the book *The Sham Squire, or The Informers of '98* that Dowdall was present at the alleged midnight burial of Emmet in the old Glasnevin cemetery. Such a burial was not recorded in the church records. Mr. Quaid commenting on this reference said "If we find Mr. Fitzpatrick's (the author) second-hand version of the alleged midnight burial in Old Glasnevin inaccurate in one respect, may we doubt its correctness in its entirety.

Mr. Quaid commenting on the funeral of Mrs. Emmet on the 11th September 1803 a few days before her son was executed posed the question as to who would have been present at her funeral. Very few he felt would have had the courage to publicly associate themselves with the Emmets because of Robert. There may perhaps have been her daughter Mary (Mrs. Holmes) whose husband Robert was by then in jail. Mrs. Patten may have been there as her husband John was in prison, he being a brother-in-law of Thomas Addis Emmet (Robert's brother). The only connection of Emmet's to have been free was Dr. Powell married to a cousin of Robert's and either or both of them may have attended. Possibly Leonard, the gardener to the Emmets would also have been present although it would appear that this was not mentioned to Dr. Madden when he interviewed him in 1836.

Mr. Quaid in his book stated that in his opinion the secret of Emmet's interment was in the keeping of Robert Holmes "and well did he keep it." He based this on a number of factors. Robert Emmet's father Dr. Robert Emmet made a will dated 3rd February 1800 and appointed his son Thomas Addis Emmet as his executor and trustee. The latter was then a State prisoner in Fort George, Scotland following the 1798 rebellion. On his release he went to Paris and from there to the USA never again returning to Ireland. There was an undated codicil to the will which stated:

ROBERT HOLMES – *Brother-in-law of Robert Emmet.*

"In case it should be inconvenient to my son, Thomas Addis, to act as my executor as by the within will appointed, I then and hereby appoint my son-in-law Robert Holmes, Esq. to that trust." As Thomas Addis Emmet did not return to Ireland, Robert Holmes held a very important position with regard to the Emmet family as it was he who saw to the carrying out of the administration of Dr. Emmet's estate. Because of this there is no doubt but that there was considerable correspondence between Holmes and Thomas Addis Emmet. The question of his brother's last resting place must have been dealt with, yet not a single piece of documentary evidence regarding this has ever come to light.

Mr. Quaid also pointed out in his book that Robert Holmes was all through his life the trusted friend of the Emmet family. He was their confidant and adviser and Quaid maintained that surely Holmes would have been asked by Thomas Addis Emmet to have the remains of his executed brother placed in the family vault with his parents if he knew where those remains were. For Mr. Quaid to come to that conclusion he was assuming that the remains had been lifted from Bully's Acre and placed elsewhere by some relation or friend until a favourable opportunity arose to have them placed in the family vault in St. Peter's churchyard.

Mary Holmes, Robert Emmet's sister died in 1804 and as stated by Dr. Madden in the second edition of *A Memoir of Emmet* published in 1860 "her remains were interred with those of her parents in the churchyard of St. Peter's church, Aungier St." Mr. Quaid commenting on this in his own book asked the question "Why did Holmes not inscribe the tombstone, if there was one, to her memory? Is it not clear that he desired the family grave to remain in obscurity and so allowed it to remain for fifty years while he was in Dublin (he died in 1859) in order that to the very letter he might comply with the testament of the patriot?"

Robert Emmet's wish was that he be left in oblivion until Ireland took her place among the nations of the earth. His statement did not imply that it should be forever, as Mr. Quaid appears to have interpreted the closing lines of the speech from the dock.

Mr. Quaid's reasoning that St. Peter's churchyard was really

Robert Emmet's resting place was based on the fact that Mrs. Holmes (Emmet's sister) who died in 1804 while her husband was still in prison was secretly buried there, this secret burial indicating that Emmet's remains had already been in the family vault or that they were placed there at the same time as those of his sister.

Although Robert Holmes was in prison, he had all the privileges of an untried prisoner and would have been able to give clear instructions while inside as to his wife's burial and if necessary for that of his brother-in-law Robert Emmet. There was no church record available of the burial of Mrs. Holmes at St. Peter's and records were also examined at St. Michan's and a number of other churches. Mr. Quaid felt that there was a deliberate concealment of Mrs. Holme's burial and made the following assumption in his book:

> "Why should all this secrecy have been necessary when Mrs. Holmes was being interred in St. Peter's in 1804. . . . The only answer is that the exhumation of the remains of Robert Emmet as incontestably shown by Dr. Madden took place at the time Mrs. Holmes was being interred. If this was so, the patriot's remains must have been laid with hers in the unmarked grave of their father and mother in St. Peter's . . .

It was a reasonable assumption but all that can be said in its favour is that it was an assumption and nothing more. Where did the body lie in the meantime is a question to be answered? It will be recalled that Dr. Madden was told that following the burial in Bully's Acre the remains were later taken from there and buried in St. Michan's. This episode was also mentioned in *The Sham Squire and the Informers of '98* by Fitzpatrick who referred to an interview with John Patten as follows:

> "We had the pleasure, soon after, of a conversation with John Patten, then in his eighty-seventh year. This gentleman was the brother-in-law of Thomas Addis Emmet. He told me that having been a State prisoner in 1803, he was not present at Emmet's funeral. He had no authentic information on the subject but according to his impression, Robert Emmet had been buried in Bully's Acre – also known as the Hospital

> Fields; and that the remains were thence removed to St. Michan's Churchyard where the ashes of Bond and Sheares rest. He added that Dr. Gamble, the clergyman who attended Emmet in his last moments, was a very likely person to have got the remains removed from Bully's Acre to St. Michan's. The uninscribed tomb is said to have been set up in St. Michan's Churchyard soon after the period that Mr. Patten believes the remains of Emmet to have been removed from Bully's Acre . . ."

Again this is pure hearsay and as John Patten stated he himself had "no authentic information", and there was never any reference to this from the Rev. Gamble regarding St. Michan's.

The comments and observations of Mr. Quaid which form the basis of this chapter went further when he stated in his book that

> "The claims of St. Michan's and old Glasnevin are untenable. I think I am correct in saying that St. Michan's has no reliable evidence in its favour except that it was the church to which the Rev. Thos. Gamble was attached as curate . . . There is no doubt that the Rev. Mr. Gamble, who attended the brother Sheares when they died for Ireland, arranged their secret interment in the vaults of St. Michan's Church and intentionally omitted the record of their interment in the Parochial Register.
>
> Dr. Gamble was a friend of the Emmet family and we may with certainty believe he was the clergyman who carried out the re-interment of Robert Emmet. Of that re-interment there need be no doubt whatever. All other accounts agree upon this one point. Our having come to this conclusion is not, however, a justification for arriving at a further conclusion that Emmet was re-interred in St. Michan's. On the contrary, I think the discerning reader must only conclude that patriot's remains lie in St. Peter's."

Mr. Quaid's assumption left many loop holes. It will be recalled that earlier he had stated that Emmet's remains were placed in the family tomb in St. Peter's churchyard at the same time as that of his sister Mrs. Holmes. She was buried in 1804 but Emmet was executed in 1803. Where did Emmet's remains lie up to then in view of the fact that they were lifted from Bully's Acre some hours after being placed there? Were they in St. Michan's?

John Patten it will be recalled mentioned St. Michan's as the place he thought Emmet's remains were placed. He spoke about this in his eighty-seventh year. Many years earlier in conversation with Dr. Madden. Patten stated that his mother had told him that a porter in the firm of his uncle William Colville and himself (they had a business at Bachelor's Walk) told her that he had buried Robert Emmet's remains. He had, he said, taken them from the prison in Kilmainham where they had been taken after the execution and had buried them in Bully's Acre. The porter's name was Lynam, by all accounts a very trustworthy and truthful man. Subsequently John Patten heard that the body was removed to St. Michan's. There was no reference at all to St. Peter's church yard.

It would appear that without further examination St. Michan's may have been the last resting place of Robert Emmet's remains with St. Peter's churchyard in close contention. Old Glasnevin graveyard was the third location to lay claim to Emmet's remains and Mr. Quaid also assessed this.

He said that a story had been related in the book *The Sham Squire and the Informers of '98* that at a dinner party a literary friend of the author's whose name was Hercules Ellis in the course of discussion on Emmet and the uninscribed tomb stated

> "It was not in St. Michan's Churchyard but in Glasnevin and I speak on the best authority for my late father was the Incumbent there at the time and I repeatedly heard him say that he was brought out of his bed at the dead of night to perform the burial service over Emmet. There were only four persons present, two women and two men."

Mr. Quaid checked very carefully into this and could find no trace of an incumbent named Ellis at that time attached to Glasnevin and felt therefore the story to be untrue.

Dalton, the eminent historian who wrote the *History of the County Dublin* related in 1833 about his visit to Old Glasnevin churchyard. From what he wrote there would appear to have been no trace of tradition there regarding Emmet's burial. Dalton referred to the many monuments of interest and if there had been any tradition regarding the uninscribed tomb it certainly would have been strong in 1833 and Dalton would have surely referred to it.

Dealing with the claims of St. Michan's, Mr. Quaid discounts them for a number of reasons. An article in the *Journal of the Association for the Preservation of the Memorials of the Dead* had stated without any proof that the large altar-shaped monument near the wall in St. Michan's was an Emmet family monument. Quaid pointed out that given the list of Emmet family recorded in St. Peter's church records "that no more fallacious proposition could be put forward than there was an Emmet family monument in St. Michan's churchyard." He also quoted from the *Memoirs of the Emmet Family* by Dr. T.A. Emmet grand-nephew of the patriot who, it will be recalled, came to Ireland in 1880 to undertake some research. In those memoirs Dr. Emmet wrote:

> "The fact that Mr. Gamble was the Assistant Curate in St. Michan's Church is the only plausible reason which can be advanced in support of the plea that Robert Emmet was buried there where a large flat uninscribed stone is said to cover his grave. If the body could have been gotten into town it would naturally have been taken to St. Peter's church, for it was well known that the family had a vault there and that Robert Emmet's parents had been buried there but a short time before. No good reason can be advanced for a selection of St. Michan's Church with which the family had not the slightest connection."

While Mr. Quaid's book showed an excellent knowledge of the history of the Emmet family, he was adamant in coming to the conclusion that the remains of Emmet rested in the family vault. However, when one examines his book in detail and his methodical and concise examination of the data surrounding Robert Emmet's final resting place there was much assumption but very little fact as to why he should come to the conclusion he had done.

As already mentioned, he was fully convinced that it was Emmet's brother-in-law Robert Holmes who held the key to the burial saga. If that was so it must be asked why all the secrecy especially after the political storm had blown over and why hadn't the Emmet family any documentary proof to pass on?

Chapter 4

THE CENTENARY SEARCH

As the centenary of Robert Emmet's death drew near, Dr. Thomas Addis Emmet of New York was urged through letters from many interested sources to initiate a further search into the location of the remains of the executed leader of the 1803 rebellion. He complied with their wishes and came to Ireland in 1903. His son Robert travelled with him. Dr. Emmet later recorded the searches that he had carried out in a book called *Incidents in My Life* but prior to doing so he related in detail some circumstantial evidence which had been more or less accepted by succeeding generations of the Emmet family in America with regard to the burial place of the 1803 leader.

Dr. Emmet said that since childhood he, above all the Emmet descendants, had the greatest interest in the life of Robert Emmet learning from his own father, and grandfather, his uncles and aunts all about him. They had known him and Dr. Emmet always felt that they most have been familiar with the circumstances surrounding the final burial place. However, he did say that he could not recall ever hearing the subject of Robert Emmet's burial being discussed but it was assumed that he was buried in an unmarked grave as was his wish in his famous speech from the dock. To Dr. Emmet's knowledge no doubt had ever been cast on this assumption until all those who would have had any knowledge passed away. There is no evidence of course that any of Dr. Emmet's predecessors really ever knew the facts surrounding the patriot's last resting place.

Dr. Emmet went on to relate in his book that the existence of the family burial place in St. Peter's churchyard was known to every member of the family before publication of Dr. Madden's work referred to earlier. It was equally well known to the Emmet family that several of Robert's brothers and sisters including his brother Christopher Temple Emmet his eldest brother were interred there before the death of their father. The church burial records confirmed this. However, Dr. Thomas Addis Emmet also stated that the body of Robert Emmet's mother was placed in the family tomb a few days before his execution as was that of his sister, Mrs. Holmes a year later. These two were not recorded and yet there was another recorded burial in 1813. This was the last recording. Dr. Emmet went on to say in his book:

> "It must also have been known later to the children of Thomas Addis Emmet (Robert's brother) that at the time of their uncle's execution every male member of his family, near relative or connection was dead, in exile or imprisoned, so that in consequence of this and the disturbed state of Ireland, it was impossible to place his body then in the family vault. But after the release from prison of Robert Emmet's brother-in-law, Mr. Robert Holmes and of Mr. John Patten, the brother of Thomas Addis Emmet's wife it must have been learned from Rev. Thomas Gamble, a connection of the family and assistant curate at St. Michan's church, of his disposition of the body of Robert Emmet after he had removed it from the Gate-House of Potter's Field, Dublin on the night of the execution."

This statement regarding 'the Gate House at Potter's Field' Kilmainham differs from what had been the accepted story at the time of Emmet's execution which was that when Emmet's body wasn't claimed, it was buried in Bully's Acre in Kilmainham. This, it will be recalled, was confirmed by Dunn the jailer when Dr. Madden was conducting his search in 1836. It was also referred to by John Patten. Dr. Emmet appeared to have ignored this by saying that the Rev. Gamble removed the body from the Gate House and buried it elsewhere thus implying that there had been no initial burial at Bullys Acre. Dr. Emmet went on to say:

> "It cannot be supposed that these two gentlemen, who were men of great prominence and living for over fifty years in

> Dublin after that event, remained ignorant of the disposition of their relative's body nor is it possible that, had there been any doubt in the minds of his relatives in New York, that Robert Emmet's body had not been finally placed at rest with his father and mother, the fact would not have been discussed; for, even before the death of Thomas Addis Emmet no reason for secrecy any longer existed. All the facts must have been known to at least ten members of the family, the last of whom did not die until the writer (Dr. Thomas Addis Emmet) had passed middle age."

And yet, is it not strange that not one iota of data came from any of those ten members of the Emmet family positively stating where the remains of Robert Emmet lay? Dr. Madden knew most of them yet we are led to believe that they allowed this highly esteemed and respected man to search for an answer that they already had. Is it also not strange that no record was kept that would allow the patriot's tomb be inscribed when Ireland took her place among the nations of the earth. Dr. Emmet stated that at the time he himself was making enquiries no one then living actually knew when the body of Robert Emmet was removed from the receiving vault of St. Michan's church where it was believed to have been placed by Rev.Gamble. The use of the word 'believed' again casts doubt over the entire story to date.

As earlier mentioned neither Robert Emmet's mother nor his sister Mrs. Holmes' burial in the family vault in St. Peter's churchyard was recorded. Why Mrs. Emmet's burial was not recorded is difficult to understand as she was buried before her son's execution. The situation with regard to Mrs. Holmes is somewhat different. Dr. Emmet in his book *Incidents of My Life* stated that it was known that Robert Emmet's sister was for some unexplained reason buried in the family vault at a late hour in the night. He posed the question in his book

> "Why could it not have taken place, as was the usual custom, publicly and in daylight. Is it not a natural inference, in the absence of any other known reason or plausible theory, for so unusual procedure, that the same hour and place were chosen for the removal of her brother's body and for its final interment

Dr. Madden pointing to the supposed grave of Robert Emmet in Glasnevin.

in the family tomb? The lateness of the hour and the darkness, combined with the necessary opening of the vault would have made the transference of Robert Emmet's body and its burial feasible in the secrecy and the avoidance of public disturbance."

There is little substance in what Dr. Emmet wrote in his book regarding the burial of his grand-uncle, and down through the years afterwards not one shred of documentary or substantiated oral evidence could be produced by any one of the Emmet family or their relatives to support what supposedly had taken place.

We now return to Dr. Emmet's search in the centenary year 1903, a search that was very detailed. It will be recalled that Old Glasnevin cemetry was one of the suggested locations of Emmet's remains. When Dr. Emmet had previously visited Ireland in 1880 he had met Dr. Madden who, he said, was then a very old man. Madden had actually given him some correspondence at that time. One of the letters, written in the 1830s had been from the Rev. Patrick Carroll, rector of the Protestant parish church of Glasnevin in answer to an inquiry by Dr. Madden. Rev. Patrick Carroll stated in that letter that in his efforts to clean up the churchyard on taking over the parish, he had set upright a number of headstones which had fallen and were blocking the walks around the cemetry. He recollected personally placing the stone which was popularly supposed to cover the grave of Robert Emmet, in its present position in order to get it out of the way. In other words according to the Rev. Carroll, there was no grave where the stone lay.

In an effort to do a detailed search on the two main suspected locations i.e. St. Peter's Churchyard and St. Michan's Churchyard it was necessary to carry out some exploratory excavation work and to this end permits were obtained by Dr. Emmet through Francis J. Biggar of Belfast and David Quaid, the Dublin solicitor whose book *Robert Emmet – His Birth Place and Burial* has already been discussed. St. Peter's churchyard, the Emmet family burial ground was first looked at.

The search began early on Monday morning 6th July 1903. Present were Dr. T.A. Emmet, his son Robert, the Rev. Standford

Dr. Madden in the site of Emmet family grave in St. Peter's Churchyard.

F.H. Robinson, assistant curate at St. Peter's church, Messrs Biggar, Quaid and Fuller and of course a number of workmen. A wide trench was dug towards the west along the south wall of the churchyard. The dig extended from the foundation of an old guard house to twenty eight feet beyond the supposed site of the Emmet vault on the south east part of the yard. A vault was uncovered measuring eight feet by eight and a half feet with the tops of two brick graves which were unopened. The vault, which occupied the supposed location was opened at both ends following the removal of concrete and earth which had been part of the fill in of the churchyard earlier referred to. The vault contained four coffins in a reasonable state of preservation. On two of them were coffin plates bearing different names and from the dates inscribed, it was felt that they were the last to have been buried there before the prohibitive law against any more burials there came in. Dr. Emmet stated that it probably was the receiving vault of the church. The names were not Emmet names.

In fact a search of five days yielded absolutely no other vault and so there was nothing in fact to prove or disprove the burial of Robert Emmet there. It established just one thing that assuming Dr. Madden's description as to the location of the Emmet vault in St. Peter's churchyard was correct, that at some later date it had been demolished and filled in. A large flat inscribed stone marked the location of and the opening to the Emmet vault in Dr. Madden's time. Dr. Emmet observed that if the stone had been left on site and the top of the vault had been covered over, this stone would have been found above the covering of concrete used in the fill in. If on the other hand it had been left on the ground surface it would have been found beneath the concrete by the use of an iron crowbar.

So far the search told Dr. Emmet and his team absolutely nothing. The search in St. Peter's churchyard was then suspended until the necessary permission was granted to extend the excavation much further and so to save time the team went to investigate the uninscribed grave in St. Michan's churchyard.

This had been the favoured location of Robert Emmet's remains. A distant cousin of Robert Emmet's mother, Mr. J.F.

Fuller had been looking after this grave for many years. It had never been opened. Along the central pathway was an uninscribed flat tombstone which had for many years been pointed out as that covering Emmet's grave. It was opened on the 1st August in the presence of Messrs Quaid, Fuller, Sir Lambert H. Ormsby, President of the Royal College of Surgeons, Ireland and Alexander Frazer, Professor of Anatomy. Two bodies were found in this grave. Nearest to the surface was that of a girl aged about thirteen years and at a depth of six feet below that were the remains of a man. The medical men present examined the skeleton. It was that of a male who had been at least seventy years of age when he died. The length and size of the thigh bone showed the man to have been tall and powerful. The bones were then replaced in the grave which was filled in. This proved conclusively that the grave which for so long had been ascribed to Robert Emmet did not hold his remains.

Further work was then continued in St. Peter's churchyard. The family vault was not located but under the transcept a headstone was found which had marked the grave of Christopher Temple Emmet, Robert's eldest brother. Nothing was found but this headstone on which was also inscribed the name of an elder sister. Dr. Emmet's contention was that it was possible the remains of both may have been reburied in their father's vault when it was subsequently built and that the headstone was more than likely buried where it was found on filling in the empty grave.

In an effort to preserve at least the location of this find, Dr. Emmet and family got permission to let the gravestone into the wall on the west side of the transcept and they had placed above it a large brass mural tablet with the inscription as follows:

> This wall stands over the supposed site of the
> Emmet Family vault which was apparently removed
> to make room for the foundations of the new transcept.
> Thomas Addis Emmet, M.D. of New York, and
> other members of the family have had the brass
> tablet placed here A.D. 1908.

A further search for Emmet's grave in the old Glasnevin

churchyard was carried out by Mr. David A. Quaid. The supposed grave was opened and dug down to a depth of eight feet but nothing was found.

Dr. Thomas A. Emmet's searches in 1903 proved that the claims apportioned to St. Michan's and Old Glasnevin as the holders of the remains of Robert Emmet were invalid and they actually revealed little more than what the family already had believed down through the years namely that St. Peter's churchyard held the patriot's remains. There was of course no proof whatever to support that belief. Dr. Emmet and his son returned to America leaving any further investigations in the hands of his relative Mr. Fuller.

Chapter 5

THE OTHER SIDE OF THE STORY

From the story so far unfolded the reader has been left with a great deal of assumption and generalisation but little to substantiate any claim that Emmet's remains lie in the family vault at St. Peter's churchyard. We know what was handed down from one generation of the Emmet family to the next.

But because of all this vagueness can it not also be said that the remains of Robert Emmet may never have been placed in any churchyard? What then if that had been the case and if so where were the remains laid and why? This book puts forward the theory that there was a deliberate policy by the Dublin Castle authorities to have the remains hidden for ever so that Emmet's grave could never become a patriot shrine and so that the wishes in the closing sentences of his speech from the dock could never be fulfilled.

While there is every reason to believe that Robert Emmet's remains were buried in Bully's Acre at Kilmainham, it is contended here that within a short time someone in the pay of the Castle authorities had the remains removed and placed where they would never again be found. It is intended to show that this was actually the case and that the Emmet family never knew where Robert Emmet's remains were finally laid to rest but adhered to the plausible story that they had been placed in the family vault in St. Peter's churchyard. Also that the authorities believed that regardless of questions ever being asked regarding Emmet's remains, the location of their last resting was a secret that would never be revealed.

When Dr. Thomas Addis Emmet returned to America in 1903,

Sketch of Entrance to Trevor Vault in St. Paul's Churchyard 1906

following completion of the work he had set out to do in trying to locate his grand-uncle's grave, he handed over the responsibility of engaging in any further search to his relative Mr. J.F. Fuller a very well known ecclesiastical architect. The Belfast archaeologist Mr. J.F. Biggar M.R.I.A. who also had assisted Dr. Emmet was also available, if required.

Needless to say the searches carried out by Dr. Emmet in 1903 attracted a certain amount of publicity. In fact it was this publicity that was to trigger off the recollection of an incident that occurred in 1887 when a man named Thomas Barnett was sexton of St. Paul's Church in North King St. Some minor alterations were being undertaken in the churchyard and as a result of the work in progress the entrance to a vault was disturbed making easy access to the actual vault itself. On the following day accompanied by a few colleagues Barnett entered the vault where he saw two tiers of coffins, three on each tier. With the exception of one all were of very expensive wood, some were lead lined. The exception was the top coffin at the rear which was made of very cheap material and contained a headless skeleton with a bundle of shavings in the area that would have been occupied by the head had it been there.

Thomas Barnett told the Rev. Gilbert Mahaffy rector of the church of his discovery. The rector checked the church records and found that the vault was known as the Hill-Trevor vault. In an effort to trace the owners of the vault he mistakenly contacted a family of somewhat similar name in Northern Ireland who had relatives buried in the churchyard and asked them if they could throw any light on the discovery of the headless skeleton. They couldn't offer any satisfactory explanation regarding the headless remains and accordingly the vault was again closed and there the matter rested.

Nothing more was thought about that discovery until the publicity in 1903 regarding the search for Emmet's remains which triggered off that incident in the mind of Thomas Barnett. He felt that it may be worth looking into again. He mentioned his discovery of 1887 to a private source who in turn leaked some of the particulars to a Mr. J.J. Reynolds, T.C. who was the author of a

Session House in Gaol Kilmainham

book *Footprints of Emmet* published in the Emmet centenary year. Accordingly Mr. Reynolds had an interview with Thomas Barnett and the story he was told attracted his attention and after studying the information revealed to him he wrote to Mr. J.F. Fuller, the Emmet relative referred to earlier. He in turn contacted Dr. Emmet in New York who directed Mr. Fuller to get the necessary permission to open the Hill-Trevor vault.

Some time had elapsed from the time Thomas Barnett made the first disclosure and it wasn't until the 11th July 1905 that Mr. J.J. Reynolds in a letter to the *Dublin Evening Mail* disclosed the facts as he had received them to "offer a good prima facie case for further investigation." Mr. Fuller got the necessary permission to open the vault and this was done under his direction. Among those present at the opening was Mr. Reynolds who later related what he had seen

The entrance to the vault was from the churchyard by means of a narrow opening near the surface of the ground. The stone steps by which access was obtained were almost in a direct line with the south wall of the church and fell almost perpendicularly into the vault. The vault itself was of massive stone construction with an arched roof measuring about twelve feet square. The walls and floor were perfectly dry although the coffins seemed to have suffered somewhat from the effects of damp which probably happened following the accidental opening of the entrance to the vault some eighteen years earlier. Thomas Barnett the sexton had then found the wood of the coffins in a much better state of preservation.

The vault contained six coffins which were located in two tiers, placed lengthwise against the wall which faced the entrance steps. The walls to the left and right were unoccupied. The tier at the back rose to a height of some four and a half feet from the floor of the vault. The coffin on top of the back row and close to the wall was in an exposed position. Its appearance was in every sense remarkable. Describing it in a letter to the Evening Telegraph dated 31st October 1905 Mr. J.J. Reynolds said:

"It was of an entirely different character from the others in the vault, being unmounted and of the plainest and poorest description. The timber was only half an inch thick and there was no trace of lining in the interior. It was to all appearance a pauper coffin, such as would have been put together in workhouse or jail. Through the effects of time the woodwork had become corky and spongy and broke away to the touch. But the most extraordinary circumstance in connection with the investigation is the fact that the skull was missing and the cavity where the head should have been was occupied by a large bundle of shavings which upon examination were found to be of the same material as the coffin."

The shavings had become so discoloured by time as to present on first looking, the appearance of a heap of dark seaweed. The shavings in fact had become practically part of the sides and bottom of the penal coffin, establishing that they were placed there at the same time as the body.

In order that the examination in the vault would be completely above board and that every detail recorded, Mr. Fuller invited along two eminent Dublin surgeons Sir Lambert H. Ormsby, Past President, Royal College of Surgeons Ireland and Professor Alex Frazer, Professor of Anatomy, also of the Royal College of Surgeons. It will be recalled that these two men assisted Dr. Emmet's investigation into the grave at St. Michan's cemetery in 1903. Mr. T.F. Geoghagan photographed the interior of the vault. The surgeons carried out an examination of the headless skeleton and issued a report in due course as follows:

On Thursday, August 10th 1905, at the request of Mr. J.F. Fuller, who accompanied us, we proceeded to St. Paul's Church, Dublin and entered a vault which had been opened by permission of the rector.

On entering the vault, which is built under the church and which, we were informed belonged to the Trevor family, we discovered a headless skeleton in very good preservation, in a thin deal shell, which had nearly crumbled to pieces from age, but enclosing this skeleton intact, save that the skull and lower jaw were missing.

As the result of careful examination, we are in a position to state:-

1. That the bones belonged to a young male of medium height and between 20 and 30 years of age.
2. All the cervical vertebrae were complete and never been subjected to any great violence, which is proof that the head was not severed from the body with an axe; but whether it was cut off by an expert with a knife or sword, or removed by other means, we are not in a position to say; nor is it possible to determine whether it was removed soon after death, or fell away by the natural process of decay.

The surgeon's report dealing with the age and height of the skeleton fitted in to Robert Emmet's category who was twenty five years of age when executed and who was of medium build. With regard to the cervical vertebrae being undamaged, the removal of the head with a knife was usual following execution at the time of Emmet. A verification of this was that in 1842 Dr. Madden examined the vertebrae of the Sheare's brothers in St. Michan's cemetry, executed for their part in the 1798 rebellion and found that "there was no injury to their cervical vertebrae." A contemporary account of Robert Emmet's execution given by a Mr. Flanagan who had at one time been a member of Alderman Carleton's Yeomanry Corps in Dublin in 1803 and who was present at Emmet's execution stated that "when he (Emmet) was hung the executioner cut off his head with a knife."

On completion of the examination of the remains in the Hill-Trevor vault it was again sealed. Mr. Fuller forwarded the findings to Dr. T.A. Emmet in New York.

In the meantime, the discovery of a headless body in the Trevor vault got considerable publicity in the press through Mr. J.J. Reynolds. The Dublin solicitor David A. Quaid whose observations and comments on Robert Emmet's burial place have been dealt with in an earlier chapter took issue with Mr. Reynolds on publishing what was discovered in the vault and declared it to be inaccurate. Mr. Reynolds wrote a reply in which he said:

> Mr. D.A. Quaid, although not present at the investigation, appears to have formed the opinion that any statements made without his fiat must necessarily be inaccurate. As I am

convinced that the subject is of too pathetic and sacred a character for anything in the nature of an acrimonious controversy in the public Press, I shall rest content with saying that I have merely stated the facts as they came under my personal observation and of course, do not require Mr. Quaid's authorisation in doing so. I feel convinced that the remains are those of Robert Emmet, a view which is shared by Mr. Fuller.

It will be recalled that Mr. Quaid in his book published in 1902 showed himself to have his mind fully made up, regardless of what evidence came to hand, that Robert Emmet's remains lay in the family vault in St. Peter's churchyard. It will be shown later that his many assumptions were those of a man with tunnel vision as regards Emmet's burial place.

With reference to the Hill-Trevor vault where the headless body was found, it is very clear that the remains were not of an ordinary political offender. After all, they lay unrecorded in the private vault of the Medical Superintendent, Dr. Edward Trevor. The remains of the other five were recorded. A close study of the United Irishmen period would reveal that Robert Emmet's remains could not have been disposed of without the knowledge of Trevor.

The story of Dr. Trevor in Kilmainham shows that he had considerable antipathy towards Emmet and his colleagues and was very well placed to get rid of Emmet's remains for a price if he had been asked to do so or even if he had suggested it himself.

One who suffered very badly in Kilmainham while a State prisoner there with Emmet was his cousin St. John Mason. As referred to earlier this young barrister was not in sympathy with Emmet's rebellion but nevertheless was arrested and lodged in jail. There he spent two years without trial in very bad conditions and had bitter experience of Trevor's authority.

In 1807 a pamphlet appeared called *Pedro Zendono, the Inquisitor of Kilmainham*. It was widely believed that its author was St. John Mason. In it the author addressed Trevor as follows:

> "Come forth thou patron of thieves, robbers and hangmen, thou suborner of perjury, thou double adulterer."

By all accounts Trevor had more than a passing interest in the ladies and engaged in many amorous encounters, some of them in the most unusual locations such as the Sheriff's execution room in Kilmainham. As a result of one such adventure, the lady involved found herself in a 'delicate condition' But Trevor was up to the occasion and devised an ingenious plan with the assistance of the gaoler George Dunn. The latter was no angel and was more than anxious to advance himself in the prison service by whatever means. Trevor knew this and with the unique authority he wielded in Kilmainham, he promised Dunn promotion if he would marry the girl on condition that both would share her favours which they apparently did. George Dunn became first Governor of Kilmainham in 1826.

So aggrieved was Mason towards Trevor that he chiefly became instrumental in having an inquiry brought forward into Trevor's activities in Kilmainham. Through representations he had made, a sworn investigation was held in the gaol in July 1804 and when Mason was released in 1807 a memorial of his case was presented to the British House of Commons. Subsequently through Mason's efforts, Trevor's conduct became the subject of Parliamentary investigation and the charges made were very well established.

There was no one better placed to conceal Emmet's body than Dr. Edward Trevor. Of all the places of concealment, his own vault would understandably prove the most secure from discovery. While it appears reasonably certain that Emmet's remains were first buried in Bully's Acre, it would have been very easy during the night for Trevor to have the body removed and brought in a covered conveyance to his own vault in St. Paul's churchyard. At that time owing to the lower level of the churchyard the vault could be made accessible without delay simply by removing the slab that was covering the entrance.

Letters continued to appear in the press following the original disclosure of the discovery of the headless skeleton. Most vociferous were those from Mr. Quaid, who made some unsubstantiated statements and at all times appeared to be unwilling to accept any view point that would diverge from his unwavering belief.

He had written a letter to Dr. T.A. Emmet in New York, a copy of which appeared in the *Mail* in January 1906 in which he showed himself to be rather antagonistic towards Mr. J.J. Reynolds who, it will be recalled, felt that the skeleton find in the Hill-Trevor vault should be further investigated. In a rather snide opening to this letter Mr. Quaid said

> "I understand that Mr. Reynolds, who recently undertook the responsibility in the public press of giving prominence to the Hill-Trevor vault fiction, was present when the vault was opened having been duly brought into the matter."

Quaid certainly felt that Reynolds was an intruder in the case and referring to the medical report from the two surgeons who examined the headless remains said that Professor Frazer had mentioned to him (Quaid) that he was quite clear that the headless skeleton showed no indication whatever of have been decapitated although the vertebrae were intact. It will be recalled in the surgeons' report that it had not been affirmed that the body had not been decapitated. Quaid also stated that professor Frazer told him that one of the thigh bones of the skeleton was diseased and as Robert Emmet was noted for his health and vigour, the skeleton was obviously not of him. It was rather strange that such a pronounced defect was not highlighted in the medical report of the eminent surgeons and such remarks as appeared in the public press were not substantiated by the surgeon concerned.

Mr. Quaid's bias again broke through in another remark against Mr. Reynolds when he stated that the headless skeleton in the Hill-Trevor vault had no significance whatever

> "until the enterprising sexton of St Paul's and Mr. Reynolds, who is a member of the Dublin Municipal Council (elected by public suffrage) forced the fiction upon the public attention."

When a copy of Quaid's letter to Dr. Emmet in New York appeared in the *Mail* , Mr. Reynolds quickly replied and took Mr. Quaid to task.

> "I am somewhat at a loss to account for the peculiar animus displayed in Mr. Quaid's letter but must conclude that anyone who brings forward any facts which question his pet theory will provoke his animosity. Mr. Quaid appears to be desirous

of arrogating to himself the sole-proprietary right of inquiry with this interesting historical question which has, during the greater part of a century, occupied the attention of all who take an interest in the pathetic story of Robert Emmet. One might expect, at least, that Mr. Quaid would approach the subject in a somewhat chastened spirit owing to his failure to prove his elaborate hypotheses regarding St. Peter's all of which have completely broken down under the test of an actual investigation in that churchyard.

"Mr. Quaid's sole argument would appear to be the 'Sphinx-like silence' of Robert Emmet's relatives . . . These relatives of the patriot lived down to the 'sixties and the historians frequently conversed with them on the subject. Neither the historian of the United Irishmen nor Mr. Fitzpatrick author of *The Sham Squire* were able to penetrate the 'Sphinx-like silence' of these gentlemen. It required the acumen of Mr. Quaid forty years after their deaths to do so. Can we believe that if Holmes and Patten had known, they would have allowed the secret of Emmet's burial place to die with them? Was ever so elaborate a superstructure built upon so slender a foundation?

"It is unnecessary to state that Dr. R. Madden over forty years ago pointed out that the family burial place was at St. Peter's and there are citizens still living who remember to have seen the stone described by Dr. Madden, consequently this cannot rank amongst Mr.Quaid's self-lauded "discoveries". . . . Even if any difference of opinion did exist as to the identity of the remains found in the Trevor vault, the statement which has appeared giving the particulars of the discovery is not, as described by Mr. Quaid as "fiction" but has been proved by irrefragable evidence. It is altogether unnecessary for me to discuss any alleged statement not embraced in the surgeons' report."

Dr. Thomas Addis Emmet in New York did not agree with the views expressed in Mr. Quaid's letter on the subject of the discovery and investigation into the headless skeleton. Quaid also requested to have the letter that he had written to Dr. Emmet in

New York published there. Dr. Emmet did not do so and in a letter to the *Evening Herald* said that he had written Mr. Quaid telling him that he felt no good could come of it. He went on to say:

> "It is possible that the English Government may have wished the remains of Robert Emmet hidden away and no better place could have been selected. But no proof exists nor should any opinion be formed on the subject for or against, until some record might in time be found in the public papers of the day which would settle the matter. No one could be more anxious than I am in the desire to have the matter settled but in the absence of all proof, I cannot form any opinion . . . ."

A short time before he died, Dr. Emmet in his last published work in 1915 made the following statement regarding the headless skeleton in the Trevor vault.

> "It would require but a trifling corroboration from some other source to establish a complete chain of circumstantial evidence to prove that at last the remains of Robert Emmet had been located."

There the matter ended. In the concluding chapter of this book we will look at the facts as they have been presented and assess the validity of the idea that the Hill-Trevor vault is the mystery grave of Robert Emmet.

Chapter 6

CONCLUSIONS

Although Robert Emmet's Execution in 1803 made him a hero in the eyes of the Irish people, his request that his memory be left in oblivion until another time was certainly not observed. However, although his famous speech from the dock achieved enormous fame and he himself became part of Irish history, the anniversary of his death was not commemorated. This was understandable in the early years after his execution but when the political situation settled down somewhat one would have thought that there would have been those who would wish to honour the patriot and pay tribute to him at his uninscribed tomb. Questions were asked as to its location but there was little more. So what did happen? Little or nothing until about thirty three years after Emmet's death when Dr. Richard Madden, historian of the United Irishmen sought to find his last resting place.

The most widely accepted story regarding the disposal of the remains of Robert Emmet was that as no one claimed them, they were buried in a pauper's grave at Bully's Acre, Kilmainham. It will be recalled that this fact was confirmed by George Dunn the jailer to Dr. Madden in 1836 when he began his investigation. Within a short time of being placed in that grave someone had those remains lifted and placed elsewhere. Who took them? Why were they taken? Where were they finally laid? These are questions that require answers.

One who understood the United Irishmen period was Dr. Madden. He was a highly respected man who interviewed many contemporaries of Emmet, yet he was unable to make any definite pronouncement on his last resting place. He knew and spoke to the Emmet relatives and if they had any definite ideas as to where the remains lay it is extremely likely that they would have told him thus saving him the time and effort with his search. At the time of his investigations the dust had well settled on the United Irishmen period so there was really no need for any great secrecy.

Robert Holmes and John Patten had no doubt corresponded on many occasions with Thomas Addis Emmet, Robert's brother, the former especially through handling the estate of the Emmets' father. It is inconceivable that should either of them have known where Robert Emmet was finally buried they would not have told Thomas Addis Emmet in New York. And if he had been told why was it that this was not officially disclosed to the Emmet family and relatives? What was to be gained by hiding for ever the location of Robert Emmet's burial place? After all he was the fifth member of the family to bear the name Robert, his father Dr. Emmet being so keen to perpetuate it. To deliberately bury that name for ever through secrecy would be apalling behaviour by the Emmets if that was the case.

Robert Emmet made a very famous speech from the dock on the day of his trial. It was a speech that caught the imagination of countless generations of Irish people. That speech was to be found displayed in many of the schools of Ireland in the 19th century and well into the 20th century. Much of it was quoted down through the years none more so than the closing sentences:

> "Let my memory be left in oblivion and my tomb remain uninscribed, until other times and other men can do justice to my character. When my country takes her place among the nations of the earth, then and not til then let my epitaph be written."

Can we honestly believe that one or other of the surviving Emmet relatives, after his execution, placed his body secretly in the family vault and that his brother in New York Thomas Addis Emmet knew all about it but went on with a conspiracy of silence? Did Thomas Addis Emmet himself, who had suffered imprisonment for his involvement with the United Irishmen rebellion of 1798 and who on release from prison made America his homeland see absolutely no future for Ireland ever? If that was so, then that great speech from the dock of his patriot brother as the shadow of death hung over him was all in vain. It is extremely doubtful that this was the case. Robert Emmet wanted silence and anonymity only until such time as Ireland took her place among the nations of the earth.

Yet to day there is still silence. It is not a conspiracy of silence, it is simply that there never had been the slightest factual evidence that the last resting place of Robert Emmet was known to his family, and so the best situation was to hand down from generation to generation the story that Robert Emmet's remains lay in the family vault in St. Peter's churchyard.

A full chapter in this book has been devoted to David A. Quaid's *Robert Emmet, his Birth Place and Burial* which was published in 1902 and which dealt in extraordinary detail with many aspects of the Emmet family. Yet, despite all the very methodical work that Mr. Quaid undertook, his dealing with the location of Robert Emmet's last resting place was very much flawed by his partisan approach. He appeared to have been blinded by an overwhelming desire to place the location of Emmet's remains once and for all in St. Peter's churchyard. In this he completely failed. His main theory was that Robert Holmes, brother-in-law of Robert Emmet held the key to the mystery and also that because Emmet's sister, Mrs. Holmes, was buried secretly at night that his remains were placed there at that time also.

Holmes' part in all this has been already dealt with and proved absolutely nothing. If Robert Emmet was buried in conjunction with his sister's burial, where were his remains for the twelve months following the execution? Is it not equally feasible also to say that the secret burial of Emmet's sister took place at night so that the absence of her brother's remains from the vault would not have been detected?

No one carried out a more thorough investigation into the location of the remains of Robert Emmet than Dr. Thomas Addis Emmet his grand nephew did. He came from New York in 1880 and also in 1903. It is obvious from the detailed searches he carried out that he had a very open mind about the burial location. Down through the years he had heard the story that the remains lay in the family vault in St. Peter's churchyard but it was apparent that he never fully accepted that. He in fact was the only member of the Emmet family to have really taken a serious interest in the patriot and where his remains lay. Unless he had been some what sceptical, Dr. Thomas Addis Emmet would never have bothered travelling several thousand miles to Ireland to see for himself if anything could be discovered. In fact there is little merit in the story that Robert Emmet's remains were ever placed in St. Peter's and there is no proof that any relative or friend of Emmet's knew who took the remains from Bully's Acre.

From what has been written in a previous chapter of this book the story that it was the Rev. Mr. Gamble who initially had Emmet's remains buried in St. Michan's does not stand up to investigation. If it was he who handled Emmet's remains then it would have been just as easy for him to have had them buried in the family vault in St. Peter's churchyard as it would in St. Michan's. At any rate the grave purporting to have been Emmet's in St. Michan's was opened and so the story disproved. Old Glasnevin graveyard was also disproved.

This then switches us to the theory that Robert Emmet's remains were not removed by any relative or friend but were deliberately lifted from Bully's Acre and hidden by the authorities, never to be found again. By doing this, Emmet's tomb could never be inscribed if Ireland at some stage were to take her place among the nations of the earth. No one was better fitted to have this idea carried out than Dr. Trevor of Kilmainham. His record there in many dubious transactions makes him a prime suspect.

The eminent archaeologist Mr. J.F. Fuller relative of the Emmets and who assisted Dr. Emmet with his searches in 1903 in a letter to him in 1914 commenting on the fortune Trevor left on his death asked the question:

"How did he, an illegitimate pauper and common soldier come by the huge sum of money? There is only one common answer . . . He called one of his sons Arthur Hill Trevor which would suggest relationship to the Marquis of Downshire's family of which relationship I don't know of any trace."

Further with regard to the Trevor vault, of the six coffins there, five had been recorded in the church register but none after 1797. In fact no further burials were recorded in the lifetime of Dr. Trevor who died in 1837.

While it is impossible to say categorically that it is Robert Emmet's remains that were in the sixth coffin (a penal shell) it would take very little to make a definite pronouncement. Somewhere among the papers of that period in Irish history a tiny piece of evidence lies which would finally confirm that Emmet's uninscribed tomb is in fact the Hill-Trevor vault in St. Peter's churchyard. The finding of this would at last enable the Irish people, for whom he gave his life, to write his epitaph and inscribe his tomb.

References

Memoir of Robert Emmet ... ... Dr. R. Madden

A Memoir of Robert Emmet ... ... Kinsella

Robert Emmet – His Birth Place and Burial D.A. Quaid

Incident of My life ... ... Dr. T.A. Emmet

Donahoes Magazine 1903

Whitelaw's History of Dublin 1818

Sketches of the Irish Bar ... ... W.H. Curran

Pedro Zendono – The Inquisitor of Kilmainham (Pamphlet)

Medical Report on Headless Skeleton ... Surgeons Ormsby & Frazer.

"Banba" April 1922 – The Mystery of Emmet's Grave.
J.J. Reynolds

Footprints of Emmet ... ... J.J. Reynolds

The Romance of Sarah Curran ... ... M. Barry

Prison Journal of Anne Devlin ... ... Edited by Finnegan

A History of Kilmainham Gaol ... ... Freida Kelly

Newspaper Reports 1905-1906

The Pursuit of Robert Emmet ... ... Helen Landreth

Secret Service Under Pitt ... ... W.J. Fitzpatrick